Edible Science Experiments

Children's Science & Nature

BABY PROFESSOR

EDUCATION KIDS

Science experiments are not boring when you use edible materials that kids can eat after the experiment. There are many edible experiments that can be done that will excite kids to learn. Here are some of them:

POPCORN CORNCOB EXPERIMENT

What you need: cob of popping corn, bag, microwave, to produce a hundred little starch fireworks.

Lesson: Among the four common types of corn, only one kind—which is actually called popcorn!—will pop. Popcorn kernels will explode due to the perfect drop of water inside each kernel.

Your microwave quickly raises that water to the steaming point. Then the pressure of the steam rips the kernel open and inflates the starchy mush inside.

LEARNING ABOUT EMULSIONS USING BUTTER AND WHIPPING CREAM

What you need: butter, whipped cream, a bowl and an electric mixer.

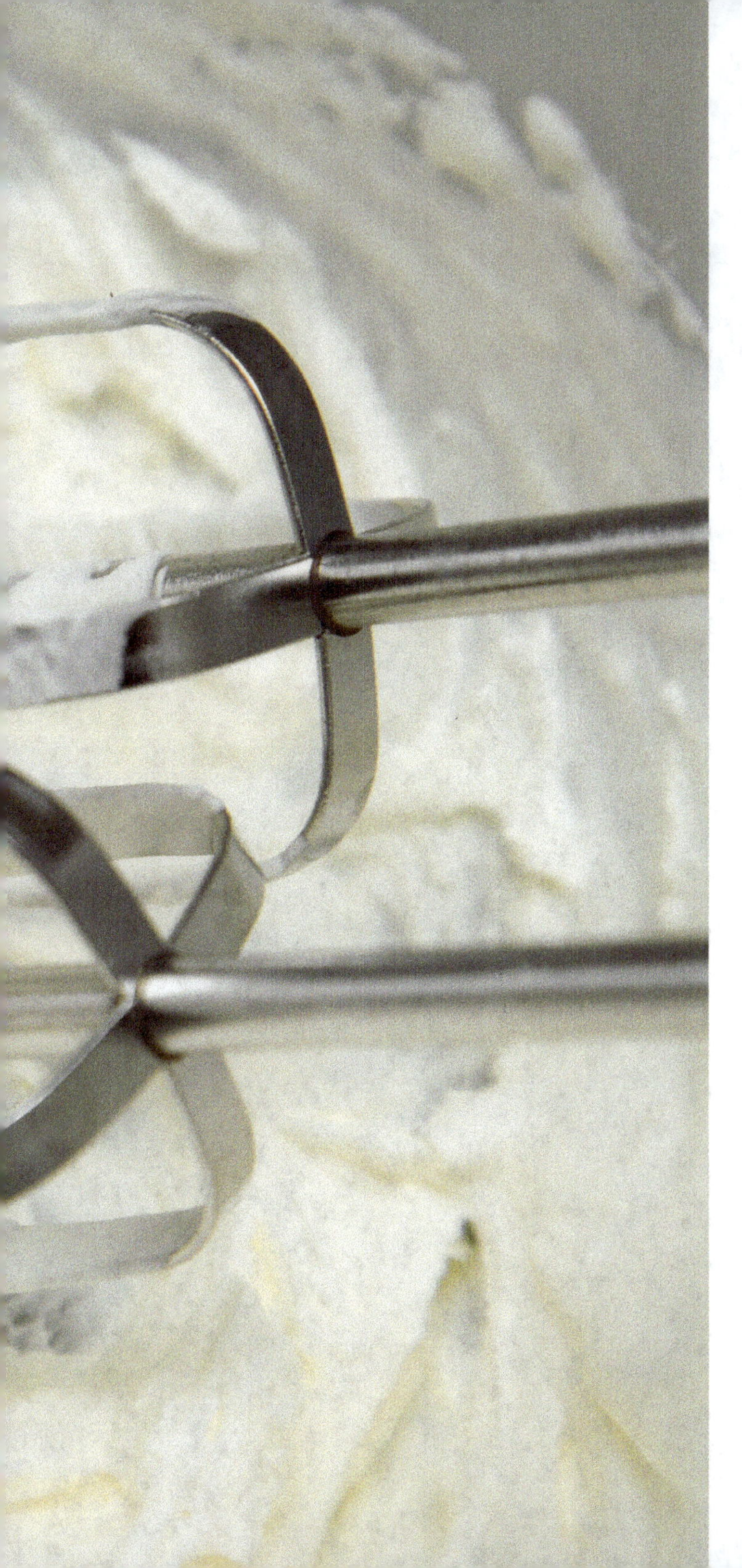

**Lesson:
Emulsion! Mixing
incorporates so
many air bubbles
into mixture, as
your cream forms
tiny protective
coverings over
the air pockets.
However, if you
don't add extra
air and just knock
all those fat globs
around, they start
to clump into the
delightful spread
we call butter.**

LEARNING ABOUT DEHYDRATION IN MAKING RAISINS

What you need: ripe green or purple grapes, a slatted tray, the heat of the sun.

Lesson:
Dehydration
happens when the
body loses a lot
of water. This is
what happened
to the grapes
when sun-dried
for two or three
days. They soon
become raisins.

LEARNING ABOUT TECTONIC PLATES AND HOW MOUNTAINS ARE MADE

**What you need:
Graham crackers,
whipped cream,
a plate, bowl
of water.**

Lesson: Spread the whip cream on the plate and place the crackers (previously dipped in water for a second to make them mushy) on top of the cream.

Lay them flat on the surface of the cream and gradually push them towards each other to see how they form a mountain. This shows how mountains are formed as the tectonic plates of the Earth slowly move and collide.

LEARNING ABOUT ACIDS AND BASES USING AN APPLE

**What you need:
five slices of
apple, five plastic
cups or other
clear containers,
vinegar, lemon
juice, solution of
baking soda and
water, solution of
milk of magnesia
and water,
labelling pen.**

Lesson: Add a slice of apple to each cup that is filled with (1) vinegar, (2) lemon juice, (3) baking soda solution, (4) milk of magnesia solution, (5) water.

Label each cup with what solution is in it. Set the cups aside for a day and then observe the difference in the discoloration of their apple slices. This will show you the effect of acidity in the process of oxidation.

Visit
BABY PROFESSOR
EDUCATION KIDS
www.BabyProfessorBooks.com
to download Free Baby Professor eBooks
and view our catalog of new and exciting
Children's Books